I0782082

VERSES OF THE
SOVIET RAIL

Peter Prizel

ISBN 978-1-968970-12-3 (Paperback)
ISBN 978-1-968970-09-3 (Hardback)
ISBN 978-1-968970-13-0 (Ebook)

Inquiries and Book Orders should be addressed to:

Leavitt Peak Press
17901 Pioneer Blvd Ste L #298, Artesia, California 90701
Phone #: 2092191548

TABLE OF CONTENTS

MOSCOW METRO SYSTEM

MAYAKOVSKAYA STATION, 1941

Located on the Zamoskvoreskaya Line, this station pays tribute to the Soviet poet Vladimir Mayakovsky. It is most well-known for its thirty-four ceiling mosaics depicting "24 Hours in the Land of the Soviets". During the Second World War the station was a command center for an anti-aircraft regiment. Josef Stalin also addressed Party leaders here as the Germans bombed the city from above in 1941.

I

A hundred feet down
trodden marble floors
reflecting a sky of peace
people, standing
against marble columns, chained
to the generalissimo, the party
organs clapping
pumping beat-red borsch
through venal tunnels
tracking timely trams
bringing in another cadre
blinded men spreading
black caviar on brown bred
looking for truths among
the red herring -smoked
corpse-like faith hangs on-
the turnstile no one dares to use.

II

The crown jewel, perhaps
the most famous
the "Man of Steel"
his namesake- arching, over

keystones in a perfect society
a day– a night– a utopia
bombed from above
till there is no one
left to lie to.

III

So here we are–
lingering
So here we are–
watching
the applause stops
Stalin smokes his pipe
telling all what to print
the morning's paper
a fictional account from below
the working class hung over
too tired to think,
ready to believe the truths–
lies tied to the tracks
waiting to be run
over by the next train.

TEATRALNAYA STATION

Named for the nearby square or the same name which features several theaters, It hall's main feature are porcelain medallions of theatrical figures, including two in profile of Russia's most famous composer: Pyotr Ilyich Tchaikovsky.

The theater, the great escape–I just divorced reality for the past
    two hours.
I watched your *Nutcracker* –was moved by a score you settled
    over a century ago,
bore witness to your masterpiece that caressed my genteel ears
    which now hear shouting.
I wait for my train to take me under the slums the subway
    tunnels– saviors,
allowing my eyes to circumvent the grinding poverty, which is
    above,
but back to the shouting down the marble hall.

Pyotr Ilyich, the men scowl at your medallion depicting your
    face in profile.
A dandy dressed to the nines stands next to man of cloth–both
    were at the show.
One spits like a contemptuous camel, the other wags his finger
    rhythmically,
like the metronome you may have used at rehearsals before you
    conducted.
I read you biography, I know your phobias, your fears–
the fact that you dreaded conducting believed it would make
    your head fall off,
the fact that you drank contaminated water–your courted death
    before you time.
A second forced marriage for you all to mask your desires.

Tried by you classmates with whom you studied the rubrics of
    law,
they weighed against you– now they do again.

I stand–waiting impatiently,
here comes the train how happy I am to escape.
Goodbye great composer, national icon.
My wish for you is for others to judge you from above,
by your sounds in the concert hall,
not from your depiction down below in the subway.
These tunnels are my saviors, alas they are not yours.

PUSHKINSKAYA STATION

This station is named after Alexander Pushkin who is often referred to as Russia's national poet. On the station's walls, one finds inscriptions of Pushkin's work. Pushkin himself died at the age of thirty-seven in a duel provoked by a fellow nobleman insulting his wife.

Routines, expectations– reprieves from the demons we are
      fighting.
The workday brought you forth from your house–you left
your quarrel with your spouse on the vine to ripen –to die.
The passage of time will tell you when– to cut the fruit–
fly down the corridor you might miss your train.

It just pulled out leaving you to spectate on the platform.
A pensioner, he haggles with a merchant over some food,
the stakes are low save for the tomatoes they talk about.
The seller paints them as the finest produce borne by the earth–
the buyer depicts them as inferior crops.
The vendor needs to unload his goods to make ends meet,
the buyer needs make tonight's supper with such items.
A woman who forgot her fare and has only a ruble asks for a free
      ride.
The station agent must decide whether to defend the State or
      magnanimity.
A youth jumps the turnstile–an officer catches him
he must decide to take the kickback or give a slap on the wrist,
whose hand will feed whom?

These are the questions at Pushkinskaya at six in the morning,
all trivial to you who are now late for work –you are drawn into
      these little duels.

Ah, how misery loves company–focus on this– try not to perse-
    verate on your woes.
Life is a series of battles of scarring, healing, and being scared
    again.
I hope yours is not too deep–here comes the next train.
I hope you left your sadness at home,
don't let these tracks be your final resting place.

TSVETNOY BULVAR STATION

This station is the closest to the world-famous Moscow Circus. Its hallmark is a huge stained glass window depicting circus performers.

You pack and unpack the same toys
you play with the same trains.
You have the same routine,
you park them- guide them
around the same circular track.
You stack the same red blocks.
You build the same towers,
you tear the same ones down–
you don't buy into the propaganda.

I wish I could
enjoy the present.
When you come to Moscow,
to see the tigers, jump through fire,
to watch the seals, beg for fish,
to laugh at the bears dance-
don't forget the clowns
those amusers–
long forgotten.

RASSAKAZOVKA STATION

Located on the Kalininsko-Solntsevkaya Line, this metro station opened in 2018. It is futurist, and its walls are filled with QR Codes which one can scan with their phone to read great works of Russian Literature. The pillars are built to resemble library filing cabinets.

We checkout every day.
From family from the office from friends,
Serve masters that renew their demands,
The grinding routine.

From family, from the office, and our friends,
a catalogue of relationships.
The grinding routine,
keeping track of obligations.

A catalogue of relationships,
a narrative arc we must follow.
Keeping track of obligations,
a moral code scanned daily.

A narrative we must follow,
unwritten but ingrained.
A moral code scanned daily,
with punctuation paragraphs and chapters.

Unwritten but ingrained,
renewed multiple times.
With punctuation paragraphs and chapters,
always in circulation.

Renewed multiple times,
often censored.
Always in circulation,
never fully filed away.

Often censored,
at times edited.
Never fully filed away,
constantly republished.

At times edited,
new editions printed,
constantly republished,
manuscripts burned.

New editions printed,
for the morning commute.
Manuscripts burned,
by the time you reach home.

For the morning commute,
from family from the office from friends.
We return on time to,
serve masters that renew their demands.

CHEKHOVSKAYA STATION

Located on the Serpukhovsko-Timiyazevskaya Line, this station is named after Anton Chekov who is considered the father of the modern short story.

You're so concise.
I envy your brevity.
Can I write like you?

MICHURINSKY PROSPEKT STATION

Named after the famed botanist Ivan Michurin, this station's entrance hall is painted red and orange and built to resemble a panorama window. The berry theme is also a tribute to Michurin who invented a hybrid of apple referred to in Russia as "The People's Apple".

I know you are anxious too.
Start school, do your best,
don't worry about the others.
Train your brain to believe.
In you we have faith,
the apple of our eye,
sees all the virtues,
the goodness,
your teacher bites,
your core must be hardened,
to track criticism as means to improve,
not as a signal of failure.
Your growth is uncharted.
You will guide us when to harvest.
Your supple mind produces,
what nature intended.

PAVELETSKAYA STATION

Built In 1950, this station is named after a railway station of the same name. The station is located on the Zemoskvoretskaya line. Highlights include a mosaic of Red Square and a painting of St Basil's Cathedral in a wooden fame near one of the exists which is under a turquoise dome.

They say old Ivan blinded the architects–plucked out their
    eyeballs.
The builders could not replicate their work, a house of God.
Who are the guests? The congregants, or the divine?
This question does not bother to enter your mind.
On your way to work you
hop the turnstile,
pull the emergency break,
disable a signal,
tempt fate,
shout
farewell,
to mourning's
lamentations of order
the social contract most of us hold oh so dear.
I know you'll say it's a union job, that the parameters are fluid.
If Ivan were around, he'd tie you to the tracks– break your work.
This station is the devil's depot–who is the host? Fellow riders
    or you?

OKTYABRSKAYA STATION

Built in 1950 to commemorate the thousands of unknown Soviet heroes who died in WWII, a highlight of this station are molded reliefs stretching through the vaults depicting images of warriors. The plates below which look like they could bear their names but are ominously blank.

Before you board remember those, who fell.
Nameless, because they were so many.
Nameless because so few are remembered.
Nameless because you won't either.
We all buy one-way tickets–
originating at the cradle, terminating at the grave.
Some lifelines are afforded more twists and turns.
Some have more witnesses.
Some are crowned with fame.
All have alibis till met by death.
Your train is late, you are frustrated.
A deal lost, a promotion passed,
means a lot to you, so Grim–
Reaper of October wheat
that fell from forgotten chaffs
unworthy to be harvested.

MARKSISTSKAYA STATION

Perhaps the reddest of all station in the Moscow Metro, Marksistskaya's architectural theme is the purity of Marxist ideals. The majority of the marble used in the construction of the station is red and pink. Main highlights of the station include single helical chandeliers, and eight-pointed stars of granite on the floor between the supporting columns.

I

Under the lamp you sit telling me you have all the answers.
Behind pamphlets and books, you preach silos of isms–
grating to my ear until I too lose my shirt–
Join the unemployed, a packrat of discontent,
ever ready to submit to your analysis of the state–
craft beer will only cloud my vision, we can talk.
I'm willing, I've still ten minutes before my train arrives.

II

We have a drink, the trains pass–
thousands of potential recruits pass–
buy their time? You pay them no heed– pass
ageway farers from other stations aren't bitter.
They've somewhere to go with their documents– pass
port of contentment. They've made a profit– I have not,
which is why I'm so ripe even when under the influence.
I look up, at the lamp, its helix doubling over,
like DNA consuming itself. It goes on forever,
reminding me that the bill of goods you speak of is just
life.

KIYEVSKAYA STATION

The station celebrates Russo-Ukrainian unity. Its pylons are decorated with socialist realist paintings of workers. At the end of the platform is a portrait of Vladimir Lenin.

The breadbasket– I don't need to live hand to mouth.
Ten years ago, I took the train from Moscow to Kiev.
You dragged me along, an unwilling caboose
inhaling the smoke from your paternal loco
to indoctrinate me to live life in the best way–
you knew how–to teach, to cajole, to influence, to persuade.
I don't blame you; you did the best you could.
If only childhood had been so easy.

Now, I'm coming into the tunnel.
I take the train from Kiev to Moscow
with my children in tow.
I disembark–look up as I wait–
my transfer is late.
I see our history –dancing on the walls.
A masquerade for the passengers,
the kids are getting restless asking when we will go.
I glance up at Vladimir Ilyich.
I understand the revolution,
If only fatherhood were so easy.

RIMSKYAYA STATION

Meaning Rome Station, this station features a sculpture complex of colorized marble columns with children playing on them as well as a fountain. At the end of one hall is a sculpture of the Virgin Mary suckling the infant Christ as well as sculpture of Romulus and Remus being nursed by a she-wolf.

On the hill to build the city, the brothers disagreed.
Through augury they staked their claims
leading to fratricide, and the founding of Rome.

You told us all that sprung from there was infernal.
You professed it to be an opium den–corrupt–
where our shadows danced mimicking false autonomy.

Now, you wish for us to bathe in its waters,
to die with her name on our lips,
to put stock in her son.

Before we get off on the wrong foot, let's have a picnic.
I'll bring the food and drinks–the easy part.
You just have to bring a new narrative–not too hard to swallow
　　　　please.

LUBYANKA STATION

Lubyanka Station is situated beneath the infamous prison (where torture was commonplace) of the same name. Here the secret police (CHEKA) was established by Felix Dzerzhinsky who employed terror to stomp out any opposition to The Communist Party. This poem also pays homage to the famous Russian ballet *The Nutcracker.*

I

Dual entrances by which to take you away.
Sweaty palms as you ride the escalator,
descending through Jurassic clay–
Stone-faced Felix gave you a pass, he has
too many screams to tame,
too many moans to minster to,
a multitude of shrieks to cater tu–
tus flare as they dance to this ballet of misery–
it is none of your concern.

II

You've reached the platform–
release the rail, walk on,
no time to curtsey.
Here comes the train,
your troop is waiting.
There's the Mouse Queen–bereaved.
Her children starved in the prison-
cell, some sugar plums so we all might shit,
our pants riddled with anxiety.
Can his long arm reach us?

III

Or are we nuts that are too hard to crack?
Sit down next to the drunk, the Holy Fool.
Hardy souls ride out from under this square.
Circles of souls above must pay for their crimes.
The whip cracks, the irons hiss, branding the skin–
deep into the tunnel we go, two exits
to make our escape.

PLOSHCHAD REVOLYUTSII STATION

Located on the Arbatsko-Pokrovskaya Line, this station is named after Revolution Square. The closest station to the Kremlin, this station has seventy-six people flanking the station, as well as their service dogs. Some of the sculptures including the nose of the dog, and the pistol of one of the soldiers, are rubbed frequently. They are reported to bring good luck.

I

The alter-ego supports the arches of the terminus.
The miner, the laborer, the solider, the partisan.
The perfect man the perfect woman ask: Why?
Why do you walk under Lenin's tomb doubting?
Rub the dog's nose, give the scent of prey,
material instincts run down the platform,
chasing your abstract dreams onto the tracks.
You want to grow wealth out of the air.

II

The miner he dug– for you.
The laborer he manufactured– for you.
The solider risked his life– for you.
The partisan he shot–for you–
are now bleeding, I see the stains.
Was it worth it to betray the revolution?
Your ID sure thought so.

III

Quick here comes the train,
get on board before you change
your mind isn't captive yet.
Let the passengers judge,
your physique–your back
your arms–your shoulders
your chest–caves
under the weight
admiration leaves–
the station you left behind.

NOVOSLOBODSKAYA STATION

Thirty-two stained glass windows, created by Latvian artists, of geometric motifs as well as those of socialist realist images, can be found in this station. The glass that was used to create these windows was originally meant for a cathedral in Riga. At the end of the hallway on a wall is a mosaic of a socialist realist woman holding up a baby who is reaching for a dove. In the original mosaic the baby was reaching for a medallion of Stalin. This original mosaic was bricked up and nearly dismantled during Nikita Khrushchev's tenure as the Soviet leader.

I

You walk past—stains.
Street walkers, street urchins
thieves, murderers, drunks.
We weren't meant to be—
here under the streets
swept away from civilized eyes.
I look down—stained.
The sun shines through
reflections of shame—
on you-on both sides of me.
I belong near God,
not down in a grotto—
flowers don't grow underground.

II

The symbolism was milked –
the woman who gave was–
not Mary the baby she holds
not Jesus, but still—you sinners walk–
buy a ticket for my upkeep.

If cleaned, I'd be more charitable,
but for now, I'm the prodigal son.
The train in is pulling out.
I don't where you are headed,
perhaps to Petersburg then
maybe on to Riga.
If you do get there,
to my hometown,
stop–by the cathedral,
pray for me as I do–
for you.

ELEKTROZAVODSKAYA STATION

This station is named after the electric lightbulb factory that was nearly. The ceiling of the station is covered with six rows of iridescent lamps (there are 318 in total). Another notable feature are the bas-reliefs which depict struggles of Muscovites during World War II.

Under the clock–wise people meet–the timing is beautiful.
They read the paper; they sip their coffee.
The banality of life on full display.
The bas-reliefs go to sleep, the war is over.

Under the sickle the people slip
like chaffs of wheat in the wind.
The train passes–papers fly, coffee spills.
The bas-reliefs awake, has there been an invasion?

Under the hammer, people tremble.
Brow-beaten nails hold track trestles.
The signal changes– crash– an accident.
The bas-reliefs rush to help.

Under the Soviet-unions gather.
Like groups of ants, they work.
Lives depend on it–the stations shut.
The bas-reliefs finish up –

Under the counter-clockwise turns look ugly.
What has changed– the way you put in the light bulb?
318 shine down– soft light on a bad situation.
The bas-reliefs look down–saddened.

AVIAMOTORNAYA STATION, AT 23:30

This station pays homage to aviation, a massive propaganda tool during the Stalinist years. The ceiling consists of upside-down gold pyramids and the statue at the end of the hall shows Icarus flying over ascending airflows.

When did flight become the answer?
When man saw the ground as an affront to dignity.
"He will cover you with his feathers,"
that's what he was told –
still, he does not believe,
Icarus has to fly.

Over airflows underground he perches.
Commuters pass,
holding the briefcase for the wings painting propaganda
in hues of blue, red, green, and smatterings of gold.
They plaster upside down pyramids – duping the Eye of Horus,
through layers of ceiling dust brought back the from the moon.
Now the youth has reached too far– the king glances upward,
both are history– in the underground metropolis–the trains still
    run on time.
The earth still spins on its crooked axis of 23 ½ degrees,
people still have to go to work.

DOSTOEVSKAYA STATION

Located on the Lyubinsko-Dimotrovskaya line, this station opened in 2010. It depicts scenes form the works of the famed novelist, Fyodor Dostoevsky including one of the murder from his famous work *Crime and Punishment*.

I am new edition to the age-old
    Crime –
murder–the first wrong by man to himself.
    Punishment–
the axe goes down, ghosts haunt the tracks.
    Demons–
play dice in the grey marble corridors.
    The Gambler–
forgot how much to wager this commute.
    Poor Folk–
they see the author's long, pensive face.
    The Idiot–
he forgot how big his audience would be.
    The Insulted and Humiliated–
that it would outlast him and the 237 miles.
    The Eternal Husband–
chases his wife and mistress down the escalator.
    The Land Lady–
collects your mind's hopes, dreams, unfinished business.
    The Double–
agent publishes a mass-market paperback.
    The Crocodile–
cries salty tears to rub in the wounds.
    An Honest Thief–

snatches the wallet.
  A Gentle Creature–
he let you go with your life.
  Notes From the Underground–

ON THE CIRCLE LINE

you hear a man's voice on the trains going clockwise.
You hear a woman's on those running counter–
intuitive reasoning delayed our metro's start.

The clergy said
the image of God
should not go
underground.
Perhaps they should have consulted
Dostoevsky's *Notes from the Underground*.
Now on the trains, you hear a man's voice
over the intercom as you approach the center of the platform,
a woman's voice as you leave it.
The word on the street is the man encourages one to work harder,
the woman's makes the commuter to relax on the way home.
Is life really that determinist?

←----------------St. Petersburg/Moscow----------------→

THE LEV TOLSTOY TRAIN

This commuter train is named after the great Russian writer Lev Tolstoy who served in The Crimean War. He also wrote masterpieces such as *War and* Peace and *Anna Karenina*. In the latter work, trains feature prominently as a destructive and death-causing phenomena. This overnight train runs between Helsinki, Finland, and Moscow, with a stop in St. Petersburg. It features a dining car reminiscent of Tolstoy's era.

Helsinki------------------------------St.

    Petersburg---------------------Moscow

Sip tea with me-------------------------->To

    stay awake------------------> Write:

along the expanse ---------------------->under

    the stars ----------->*Happy families*

the birches roll on --------------------->watch-

    ing you------------>*they are all alike*

as you turn------------------------------>pull-

    ing------------->*every unhappy family*

the lever --------------------------> pivot-

    ing----------->*unhappy in its own way*[1]

the Samovar----------------------->creating

    -------------------> ***Travelers–left***

boiling water----------------------->burn-

    ing ***and***--------------------> ***entered***

serpentine steam------------------->hiss-

    ing at----------------------->***our car***

---

[1] First set of four lines of italics in the third column are first lines from Tolstoy's *Anna Karenina*.

intertwined----------------------------> half-

    truths---------------->*at every- stopping*[2]

with smoke-------------------------> utter-

    ing----------------------->*All is quiet*

from a pipe-----------------------> dream-

    ing---------------------> *in Moscow.*

a yearning------------------------> a con-

    science-------------> *The squeak of wheels*

to be sucked ----------------------->dry---

    ---------------------->*seldom heard*[3]

---

[2] Second four lines of italics in the third column are first lines from Tolstoy's *Kreutzer Sonata*

[3] Third set of four lines of italics in the third column are fist lines from Tolstoy's *The Cossacks*

THE ST. PETERSBURG METRO SYSTEM

ADMIRALTEYSKAYA STATION

Located on the Frunzensko-Primoskaya line, this station pays homage to the city's naval history. Mosaics of Tsar Peter I founding the admiralty and standing near two warships can be found along with one of Neptune riding white horses. Another mosaic featuring the flag of the Russian navy can be found with cannons and anchors. The station itself is comprised of polished granite and blue stone to resemble a crystal body of water. The subway station is also the deepest one in the city, and the second deepest in the world.

Delve down another league and you will find reverence,
not a watery grave to a navy flying the banner of St. Andrew.
A fleet on the run exiled from its ports.
Old Man Winter nipping like hounds after a scent on a hunt.
What morality rides the waves, and guides the sailors on the
    high seas?
Loneliness the letter of marque, the license to lust for many a
    man–
months at sea seem like years as they venture across the endless
    blue plain.
Neptune himself could not ask for a more loyal flock.
A band of analysts to deal with his whims, his hubris, his lumps.
All for the stated purpose of protecting what is not his–

the land out of his divine reach as illusive to these mortals as
    well,
their trackless train guided by stars by maps–by a duty –I hope
    you'll never know.

AVTOVO STATION

This station pays homage to the victims of the Siege of Leningrad (1941-44). A million citizens starved to death when the city was besieged by the Nazis. A mosaic of a woman holding a child is a reminder of the lucky citizens who escaped.

I

As I walk your marble corridors–I cry.
I do not have enough tears for all.
For the baker who gave you half his ration for the day,
for the corpse I was forced to eat,
for the solider who drove me across the ice during the siege.
You weren't here during the war.
I want to dump my grief here.
In front of "Everywoman" who had a child
during those harrowing years.

II

The young commuters roll their eyes
they tell me to go
somewhere else above ground
not to stay in this Stalinist shrine
twelve meters below the Earth.
"Don't burden us with your grief.
The platform cannot hold this agenda
seventy-five years old
time to move on."

FINLAND STATION

This station is most famous for having been the venue where Lenin returned to Russia form exile in Switzerland. He came in a sealed train financed and equipped by Imperial Germany near the end of the First World War in 1917.

I'm the virus–the poison pill sent from the land who backs none,
On the sealed train, I let my theories percolate.
REVOLUTION UPON REVOLUTION THE WHEELS TURN–
Run like wild horses over dunes of certainties,
facts must be established before fiction–
narratives against human nature imprison the simple-minded
    psyche,
if an antidote is found by some lackadaisical Nike.
REVOLUTION UPON REVOLUTION THE VIRUS
    REPLICATES.
I'll mutate-stir the pot- court mass appeal to the basest of needs.
I thank you for safe passage dear Kaiser,
into the mucus membrane of a very fragile State.
Affairs between us can be figured out later,
but now let me overthrow this hallow cell,
establish it as my host lest I become the caboose of history–
REVOLUTION UPON REVOLUTION AN ELITE IS
    REPLACED BY ANOTHER.

PLOSCHAD VOSSTANIYA STATION

Meaning rebellion square, a church once stood where this station is. It was destroyed by the Bolsheviks in 1917, and now a metro vestibule is in its place. This is the only station where after de-Stalinization a bas relief of the dictator of the same name still survives.

We tried to wipe God off the map, and failed.
He is still here, a parent for the clergy and masses,
an armchair deist for high-brow scholars,
a concept, a theory for scientists.
He still on the train
of thoughts and speculations of humanity.

You tried to wipe me off the subway.
I'm still here, an icon for the old guard,
a tyrant for the clergy and masses,
a great thinker to disillusioned union workers.
I'm still at the train,
stationed next to Lenin waiting to be rehabilitated.

BEGOVAYA STATION

A highlight of this futuristic station is its propeller-like lamps. The
station is very futuristic and there is a portrait Alexander Savushkin,
a fighter pilot, and Hero of the Soviet Union.

I clipped the Stuka's wings, curtailed its murderous howl.
It landed on the icy Neva skidding past the Hermitage.
The cockpit a palace of pandemonium,
the anteroom where I was knighted a Valkyrie.

The pilot steps out unaware of his location
thinking he has landed among sympathizers
who will parrot back dictums of fascism—
a raft for his ego, as he freezes to death.

Leningrad's citizens have no time for such nonsense.
The war has pushed their minds back thousands of years,
they think of food and shelter.
Plato's *Cave*–
men have no place in the city's narrative,
they've gone off to fight,
leaving women, children, and the old
to think of nourishment for the body, not the soul.

Over St. Issacs's I fly looking for my next victim.
Mayday! I've been hit, I'm going down,
fuselage on fire no chance to live,
ejected to God in a heap of ash
from a funeral pyre bereft of mourners,
my memory memorialized in an electrified tunnel
decades after my death.
Leningrad's citizens have no time for such nonsense.

YAKATERINBRUG METRO SYSTEM

PLOSCHAD 1905 GORDA STATION,

Named after the 1905 revolution. This station is in the city where Nichols II the last Tsar of Russia and his family was murdered. The Tsars we often out of touch with their people indulging in pastimes the common person either had no time for or could not afford. One example occurred every spring when the Tsar would watch the epiphany in the river Neva from the Jordan staircase in the Winter palace, where a priest would break the winter ice symbolizing Christ's Baptism. The layout of the station is somber, with Kremlin-red granite in the center and lighter granite on the walls.

There must be an offramp,
the conductor has been signaled–
several times the passengers tried
to pull the emergency brake.

It was too much,
too much to ask,
the master of
the station.

He stands,
stands atop
The Jordan Staircase,
looking down at the frozen Neva.

He waits,
waits for the priest,
to break the ice in the water
for the epiphany.

If only
our Tsar would baptize our democracy,
not man this despotic kiosk,
leaving the passengers to render Cesar unto Cesar.

If only he'd cease,
his tunnel vision–
seals his fate
in some dark dank basement.

PROSPEKT KOSMONATOV STATION

The last station on the first line of the Yekaterinburg Metro, this station was opened in 1991 and pays homage to Soviet/ Russian space exploration. Its columns of stainless-steel turn blue in the light, and resemble rockets. Lamps in the niches of the subway walks represent portholes in spacecrafts. The chandeliers on the ceilings represent the solar system.

How the planets pay homage to the sun.
Mercury speeds by in constant genuflection.
Venus wishes her beauty its prying eyes would shun.
Mars must rein in his jingoism he's slumped in rejection.

Jupiter takes the other's kowtowing with great objection.
Saturn laughs at his son's sulking. His loins have mirth.
Uranus knocked on his side seeks primordial direction.
Neptune light years away awaits a spring birth.

Pluto's heart temporarily thawed his souls milk it for all it worth,
as he slowly guides his skiff on the rails of his revolution.
The dead call to the living they're inquiring of those still on Earth.
How does the third planet behave, what is its conclusion?
Are its inhabitants content in their station
Or did they buy tickets for cosmic liberation?

KAZAN METRO SYSTEM

KREMLIN STATION

This station is named after the Kremlin of Kazan which was conquered by Tsar Ivan the Terrible. On its platform are towers which represent the minarets of the Islamic faith which was and is practiced by Kazan's Tatar inhabitants. A fresco of a Zilant or dragon-type creature which is mentioned in legends about Kazan's founding can be found on the ceiling.

Wash my feet–I'v–an
appointment with God
on a platform.

I've a need –To catch.
To catch the train
Traveling east.

It's too late–
even on the wings of a Zilant
the Mihrab keeps moving away.

I know not which way
to pray
on innocent intentions.

The muezzin calls
from a Kremlin on high
the train schedule:

Five times
Daily
Departures.

Maybe- I'll have-
I'll have another chance
To ask–to ask for forgiveness.

If I could–I'd tie,
tie my sins,
to the third rail.

Wash my feet–I'v–an
appointment with God
on a platform–I just don't know which one.

TRAINS OF THE REVOLUTION

THE IMPERIAL TRAIN

The opulent Imperial Train was a mobile office and command center for the Tsars. It included a chapel, offices, and living quarters. It was also where Nicholas II signed his abdication whereby, he renounced his throne. This was after he refused to give his people a parliament and after he'd listened to his corrupt, and hated advisor, Grigori Rasputin, who supposedly could heal his son, and heir, of deadly hemophilia.

I'm out of touch–
I have been for over
twenty years.
On my mobile
aristocracy I hold
my pen
in my shaky
hands spilled ink.
I've broken nibs,
broken promises.

The people asked
for a parliament,
a place to flex.
Their weak mouths,
their tongues too sharp
their words too piercing
for my jealous ego
to yield
to too many opportunities
for the masses.

So, I gave them a Duma,
a place to think
a place to use
their grey matter.
But for them it was too
black and
white.
Too much power stayed
in my court,
only my words mattered.

Then my focus changed
my thoughts
shifted.
My wounded pride and
joy– my son, Alexi,
his blood drips on
the rim of death's chalice
Death wets
his lips
many times.

Until he is chased
Chased by
That mad monk
Rasputin– fathers rumors
printed in an unforgiving
penny press
making my throne
thorny as war breaks out.
I board my train,
rush to the front.

We fight bravely
countless die.
On frozen plains,
I resign,
hostage to my fate
as my people riot.
Bread!
Bread!
They scream
and strike.

In abdicating,
I stand behind
my pride.
In shame, the bad
hand deals
the nib a blow
as it glides
across the page.
I receive a standing–
O! I've been out of touch!

AGIT TRAIN

These trains were used during the Russian Revolution to spread propaganda and instill the values of the new government to the rural populace. Brightly colored, these trains often included darkrooms to develop photographs, mobile move theaters, and libraries.

Become immortalized
watch the silver screen,
we come bearing gifts.

We will show you the light–
come! Come into the darkness,
we'll wash you.

You're ripe, ripe for molding,
the black earth of your vapid
mind against a void white background.

Take your still photograph– now go.
Go into the theater, see how you might act,
under communism.

Stop at the library on your way,
there are reading lessons too.
Don't worry, we'll tell you what to read.

THE TRANS-SIBERIAN RAILWAY

THE TRANS-SIBERAIN RAILWAY CANTOS

Preamble
Vladivostok

In what was the backwater of The Russian Empire
>	where the sun rises and begins its journey across The Motherland,
Just shy of half a day, a hair away from all the steps
>	I, Alexei decided to follow upon purchasing *The Big Book*[4]
>	from a sailor.

For too many years, he'd drowned his sorrows,
>	by the naval memorial he drank spirits of the fermented.
He'd no money to buy vodka so he grew his own potatoes,
>	in the cemetery behind the bay where his fallen comrades lie

It was only when he was found passed out under
>	a blanket of snow that he took fate into his own hands.
In order to spread his gospel, he took a job as newsboy,
>	selling the *Pravda*[5] by day, violating the press by night.

Did he consider the authority of communism? It's disregard for God?
>	Did he consider the authorities? Eager to denounce all –
>	ship them to the gulag,
his fear was not enough to subdue his new truths which numbered 12.
>	Never was a clearer parable written– if he could just find a
>	willing audience.

---

[4] The Book of Alcoholics Anonymous
[5] Literally meaning "Truth" it was The Soviet Union's main newspaper

Eating potatoes by night as he works, their peels falling,
>on cheap weathered parchment they leave their fatty starchy stains.

No longer judged by their proof, but by the time-tested theories.[6]
>They contribute to nourishing the sailor's body as he tries to save souls.

He sold me the book by the train station where I purchased a ticket.
>One way to Moscow then a transfer to beyond all the way to the satellite

City of Kalingrad taken from the Germans at the end of the war.
>Through each time zone, I'll complete the eleven first steps before turning back.

To Moscow where I'll set up shop become the alter-ego of the sailor,
>preach my own gospel and complete the twelfth.

I'll start– start in third class on the train with the dregs of society.
>I'll move–move up the dozen cars till I become its conductor.

6

Car 1

(Third Class Sleeping Car)

[On the train: Step One: We admit we are powerless over alcohol.]

I've entered the house of the unwashed,
a hovel on wheels split into quarters,
two sets of bunkbeds for dreams.

A shared washbasin where I am to abdicate
my pride–admit my powerlessness.
We depart the far-east under the sun's observation.

I cannot hide anymore from Helios.
My bunkmates laugh, their ribs gyrate,
as my chest deflates and with it my conceit.

I turn the bottle toward the drain,
let its contents go to their Charybdis
to be run over by the caboose.

My bunkmates waste no time in having a wake.
They open their flasks, canteens, and nibs.
They drink, mourning my bottle–mocking my soul.

They extend an offer which would spell my end.
What was ambrosia is now poison–still my hand,
reaches only to be slapped by Divine Providence.

I chose this train because the rail is long.
But with length comes many stops.
I must stay on the wagon

I can no longer be a slave
to alcohol,
as ass to reality.

I try to sleep, to dream of sobriety.
Grant my bottle enteral rest
let my bunkmates say a never-ending Mass– I am out.

We speed though the vast taiga,[7]
my bunkmates howl at the moon,
unaware that that they cry from the lash of the drink.

---

[7] The boreal or snow forest that covers much of North America and
Russia

Car 2

(The Shower Room)

[On the train. Step Two: We came to believe a power
greater than ourselves can restore sanity.]

I.

The demon is still working its way through me,
    as I strive to give myself to God and let him take command.
        Through both ends I void –Purge as Comrade Stalin
        would have said.
            An ablution different than what I expected in the
            room of purification.
                Out!
                Out! I say! Your grasp the breath and berth of a
                holy icon. No matter
        the angle where I move–Your gaze is all-encompass-
        ing– it is all-consuming.
    I offer up all my troubles to a power greater than myself to
a one I cannot see, touch, taste, smell or feel.

II.

The water runs, runs over my back hot, like tea from a boiling
samovar.
I want to be hospitable, want to offer something to my redeemer.
I've neither bread nor salt[8]
All I have is a slate–
A fresh slate
by which to regain
freewill.

---

[8]   Traditional offering to guests in a Russian household

III.
Were grapes in the Garden of Eden?
Did Adam stomp on them?
The snake could not have.
Not outside paradise,
the serpent must move,
must move his organs,
to eat his repast.
His heart is never in
the right place.
His liver lacks reason,
but then,
so did mine.
He shed his skin in exile,
as do I.

IV.
I come before you,
a cleansed soul ready to receive,
infinite blessings.

Car 3

(The Laundry Car)

[Frist stop Khabarovsk. Step Three: We made a decision to
turn our will and lives over to God as we understood him.]

They say that cleanliness is godliness.
I watch, I watch the mad Rasputins [9] and the False Dimitris, [10]
soaking their cassocks and robes in the machines.
Does their intent equal mine?

How do they understand a God [11]they tried to dethrone?
The former took Nicholas first out his mind,
turned him into a centaur – his instinctual back to his people,
till they cut off the head of reason.

The latter travelled over the vast steppe.
Took the throne of Moscow,
until he was fired out of a cannon,
back towards Poland.

Still, they whitewash,
their past is not mine.
Nor is their present
State of affairs.

I soak my clothes,
rid my vestments of

---

[9] Russian mystic who allegedly cured the Tsarevich of hemophilia, while currying favors from the Tsar and his family, angering the people and eventually causing the downfall of the Romanov Dynasty.

[10] There were three pretenders to the Russian Throne during the "Time of Troubles" named Dimitri.

[11] The Tsar

The devil's bile as
we level with the platform.

Dock under the watch–
Ful gaze of the cathedral of
The Dormition's [12] pain–
less victory is mine.

I submit my woes,
offer my trials,
sacrifice my tribulations,
on its altar.

____

[12] Dormition refers to the idea that Virgin Mary died without suffering
and is state of spiritual peace.

Car Four
(The Library Car)
[*On the train. Step Four: Made a searching and
fearless moral inventory of ourselves.*]

How to make a moral inventory as I turn
Counter-clockwise the head on the neckless body of the doll.
Revealing sins uglier than Baba Yaga,[13]
I've no leg to stand on.

Counter-clockwise the head on the neckless body of the doll,
my transgressions are numerous.
I've no leg to stand on,
the matryoshka of sins is endless.

My transgressions are numerous,
too many sins to catalogue.
The matryoshka of sins is endless,
those I have harmed – countless.

Too many sins to catalogue,
if only I could burn their Great Library,[14]
those I have harmed – countless,
too many to name.

---

[13] A supernatural being in Slavic Folklore described as living in a
house on chicken legs and having a large nose that sticks into the
celling, and looking ugly and repulsive in general

[14] The Great Library of Alexandrea which according to legend was
burned on the orders of Caliph Omar who supposedly stated of its
books and manuscripts: "…they will either contradict the Koran,
in which case they are heresy, or they will agree with it, so they are
superfluous."

If only I could burn their Great Library.
My depravities range from petty theft to wanton deceit,
too many to name,
too many to record.

My depravities range from petty theft to wanton deceit.
They come out of the woodwork,
too many to record,
but per the book [15]expected.

They come out of the woodwork.
My transgressions are numerous.
But per the book expected,
to a now unwilling host.

____

[15] The Big Book of AA.

Car 5

(The Chapel)

*[Second Stop Irkutsk. Step Five: We admitted to God, to ourselves,
and to another human being the nature of our wrongdoings.]*

They say that for many, God is in the gutter.
But this is where I meet my Virgil[16], a monk, my tsar.
My sins were his bread and butter.
They were his own rising like steam from the samovar.

We disembark in Chekov's Paris of Siberia[17]
Journeyeto Epiphany Cathedral where we confess in both rites[18]
I was first his priest then he mine– this is how we meet the criteria,
Of step five on that cold and chilly night.

In this city known for diamonds and gold,
We discover something much more precious.
Our lives which we are beginning to take ahold,
We get them back, as hosts do not succumb to heteroecious.

We return to the train to continue our journey – humble,
in God's house on wheels, we seek not to stumble.

---

[16] Dante's guide in *Inferno* and *Purgatorio*.
[17] Checkov referred to Irkutsk as *The Paris of Siberia*
[18] Catholic churches have individual confession whereas Eastern
Orthodox have communal confession

Car Six
(The Kitchen and Galley)
[*On the train. Step Six: Were Entirely ready to have*
God remove all those defects of character.]

They say a fish rots at its head.
The cleaver comes down,
in one fell swoop severing the head of sturgeon.

Then comes the messaging – the palpating,
up and down the corpse's abdomen fingers run like piccolo player.
The chef – the Pied piper of Hamlin coaxes a black mass of eggs
        out.

Uncountable they are food fit for a king.
The chef spreads them elegantly on crackers–
Pours a cup of tea.

He exits the kitchen.
I look through its circular window.
He serves the meal to my guide and savior.

A badling monk in his fiftieth year,
ties round his neck a napkin,
preparing to take on my sins.

Oh, noble scapegoat,
my heart jumps for
joy as you lick your chops.

Have your toast,
raise your glass.
Your satisfaction is mine.

I prepare to wash my hands
To still do the work –to become clean–sober.
Under your watchful eye.

Let me join you.
In our mutual triumph,
let me have seat at your table.

Car Seven
(The Dining car with Boris)
*[Third Stop Novosibirsk. Step Seven: We humbly
asked God to remove our shortcomings]*

AL: I can see you are here on business,
in this great hub of industry.
Before you disembark, I seek your company.

BO: Your perception is correct.
    I haven't much time but sit down,
    state your needs do not genuflect.

AL: How can I but not?
    You consume my sins,
    I am indebted to you.

BO: I know not what you speak of.
    We are all sinners.
    I'm embarrassed by my gluttony.

AL: Better to desecrate the stomach.
    I've shot my liver one too many times.
    The bottle held me hostage as you know.

BO: I know you confided in me in Irkutsk.
    Have you anything else to tell me?
    As in three days we reach Moscow.

AL: Yes, where you will leave me, you have said
    I need access to the full train to each car the first-class cab-
    ins. Only you can give me that key that passage.

BO: And why is this?
> You are non the straight and narrow.
> How will you benefit?

AL: I will not be fully enlightened,
> until I complete my steps one in each car.
> There are a dozen on this train.

BO: And what will you do afterwards?
> There is the twelfth step to complete.
> To spread the gospel of the community.

AL: Exactly, which is why after completing the 11th time zone
> in Kalingrad,[19] which is as many as there are in Mother
> Russia,
> I'll return to Moscow my twelfth stop– to spread the gospel
> of which you speak.

---

[19] Russia's westernmost city, it is disconnected from the rest of the country and on the time zone nearest GST.

Car Eight
(Second Class Cabin)
*[Fourth Stop: Yekaterinburg. Step Eight: Made a list of persons
we had harmed and became willing to make amends to them all.]*

In the second–class cabin I sit,
compiling lists of apologies, we must remit.

In the Church of Blood[20] where the last Tsar as murdered,
I state my subservience so quietly, you wonder what I've murmured.

But he who need to hear has taken note,
has acknowledged the words uttered from my throat.

I return to the car and bathe in the shared bath.
A modicum of civility reigns I hear no roommate's wrath.

The bottle does exist here in the next room.
But it is kept on leash save for meals it is entombed.

Life seems peaceful but I do not rest,
I've other cars to tend to, and complete my test

Can I maintain my sobriety?
Not succumb to alcohol and all its notoriety?

Time will tell.
Through the steps my cravings I must quell.

For I still remember the demon that I washed down the drain.
It and all its minions have caused me and others undeniable pain.

––––––––––––––––

[20] Church in Yekaterinburg built on the site of Nicolas II's and his
family's murder.

I cannot remember all I've wronged, all I've harmed.
All I can do is kill the delivery method, make sure its disarmed.

Never let it rise again – rear its ugly head.
Keep try to put the nightmares it has wrought to bed.

The Tsar had to wait nearly a century to be granted eternal rest.
I'm only forty, after wandering through the desert I in contrast
    am blessed.

Car Nine
(The Engine Room)
[*Fifth stop: Perm-36 Memorial Center or Political
Repression outside the city of Perm. Step Nine: Made
direct amends to such people wherever possible,
except when to do would injure them or others.*]

Empathy is the engine of humanity being civil to one another.
My savior and I disembark at Perm.
Under the shadow of Stalinist architecture, we hail a car.
As we make our way to the gulag,
the pines bow under the snow in reverence
weeping needles in the wind.
Their tears blanket the timber huts of the victims.
I still hear their cries begging me
to stop drinking, catering to all malicious acts that grab–
the coattails of an addict are long,
they cannot be cut till he or she is ready to take the plunge.
I doff my hat in respect to graves.
They have no corpses or memory of names long gone.
They froze in minus forty-degree temps.
While I drank and had a false sense of warmth – security.
Like Stalin, I put their pleas on show trials.
Blamed them for my short comings cast them out of my life.
Or forced them into exile themselves.
To their own gulag of sorrow where they mourned the man they
        once knew.
Back in the engine room I inspect,
the values – twisted pipes, my very convoluted conscience.
Slowly, it becomes clearer.
When the train pulls away that evening from Perm, I cry.
How I wish I had a first-class cabin,
To mourn – to mourn in private. I'm granted, granted a reprieve,

when my monk goes the chapel for evening vespers.
My reality of being sober is now more pleasant than my dreams.
I've nightmares of those who are cut out from my life.
I can only ask forgiveness in my subconscious as they are dead,
literary, or have no desire to gaze upon my face.

Car Ten

(The Bar Lounge)

[*Sixth stop: Moscow. Step Ten: Continued to take a personal
inventory and when we were wrong promptly admitted it.*]

We reach our capital and thank God.
The Nazis, purveyors of our alcohol came within eighteen miles
      of it,
But for now, it seems we have stopped them.

We cross Red Square – walk at a brisk pace,
avoiding the gaze of the left's demon from his mausoleum,[21]
a mirror image of the right[22] we are fighting.

I think of those I banished as they would not heed to my
      alcoholism.
We visit the St Basil's, then the Kremlin.
It is there while in the Terem[23] that my monk succumbs.

Corruption has engulfed great Moscow.
Ladies of the night wander the streets.
He's not tempted by them but by what they drink.

---

[21] Vladimir Lenin founder of the Soviet Union an ardent embracer of
communism a far- left ideology

[22] Right-wing or fascist.

[23] A palace in the Kremlin where the Tsar's wives and concubines were
kept in the Middle Ages. On the third floor there was a bedroom
where the Tsar would select is wife from virgins who were ostensibly
asleep on eiderdowns.

As we explore the Red Staircase[24]
He succumbs to the alcohol –Like the Strelsky Guards did to
        Peter's family,
the alcohol does to his mind.

Temporarily my monk becomes elated,
maddened with ecstasy,
only to come down with a profound sense of shame.

His relapse leaves him paralyzed.
Too embarrassed to go on,
he sees me off at the train.

As it leaves, I spy the great cannon,[25]
I pray that it shoots my saviors demon out in heap of ash,
so that he may have peace in his tormented soul.

---

[24] Staircase in the Kremlin where the Steltsky rebellion took place and many members of Peter the Great's Family were thrown down the stairs and impaled on pikes from waiting Streltsky guards stationed at the bottom of it.

[25] The Tsar cannon of the Kremlin. It was only ever fired once it is history when it blasted the ashes of the pretender to the Russian throne back towards Poland where he came from.

Car 11

(First Class Cabin)

*[Seventh stop: Kalingrad. Step Eleven: Sought through
prayer and meditation to improve our conscious contact
with God as we understood him, praying only for knowledge
of His Will for us and the power to carry it out]*

We cross into Lithuania and then to Poland.
Here the gauge changes – it is narrower.[26]
I feel myself more focused, lucid–
Closer to God.

As we reach Kalingrad the gauge becomes wider again.
I must not be lured into temptation like my savior was.
In the capital of amber, I take stock. My will
power has subdued my urge to drink.

The wants become fossilized in the orange sap.
As I curate them, I am eager to return to Moscow,
to put them on display for the world to see.
So that others may follow my example.

I play, play a round of solitaire in my private cabin.
I'm reminded I cannot stay sober alone and must rely on others.
I must tame, tame my ego.
Lest I be compelled to drink again.
I pay a visit to Von Lasch's Bunker.[27]
Am I ready? I am ready to teach others?

---

[26] European railway gages are narrower than their Russian
counterparts.

[27] World War II bunker of Otto Von Lasch who directed defense of
Konigsberg (Kalingrad) before it fell to the Soviets in 1945.

I am impervious enough to temptations.
Humanity has brewed alcohol since the beginning of time.

It is not going away,
I've been through 11 cars,
been through 11 steps.
I now must commander the locomotive.

Drive the train to St. Petersburg.
Like a triumphant Lenin returning from Finland,
I must preach my gospel,
I must begin the twelfth step.

Car 12

(The Locomotive)

*[Eighth Stop: St Petersburg. Step Twelve: Having had a spiritual
awakening as a result of these step, we tried to carry this message
to alcoholics, and to practice these principles in all our affairs.]*

In the old capital I set up shop –Here I will both sell and buy.
My sobriety depends on my customers as much theirs on mine.
Near the Rostral Columns,[28] I rent my abode,
bid farewell to the iron horse who pulled me along this journey.

But just the first leg,
there is a lifetime to walk,
People to save,
rooms of salvation can be had anywhere.

From the Trubetskoy Bastion,[29]
to the throne room of The Winter Palace,
the venue does not matter,
only the souls in it.

I yearn, year to mount,
to ride the Bronze Horseman,[30]
and preach my gospel,
to lure the urchins from the subways.

From their dark hovels,
where they are blind.

---

[28] Famous russet-colored columns that act as lighthouses.

[29] Infamous prison on the Island where Peter and Paul Fortress . Here
dissents including, Peter the Great's son, Alexei, Fyodor Dostoevsky,
and Leon Trotsky were held in solitary confinement.

[30] Statue of man on a horse commissioned by Catherine II in honor of
Peter I it stamps on a serpent a symbol of treason

So, they can see the glory,
glory of a future life.

Tether your pride.
Come and hear me.
You have seen what it did to your tsar.
Don't become a footnote to history.

I've travelled thousands of miles,
To learn – teach – and learn
again, I will start the steps,
repeat them for my sake, and yours.